Rise and Fall of Inspirational Leaders

Understanding the Silent Killer of Once-Shining Leaders Switching From Greatness to Mediocrity

ISBN: 978-1-0690806-0-8

Disclaimer: The information contained in this book is provided for general informational purposes only and does not constitute professional advice. The author disclaims any liability for any errors or omissions in the content of this book.

First Edition

Contents

Chapter 1: The Burning Flame........................ 6

Chapter 2: The First Flicker.........................10

Chapter 3: The Slow Burn.......................... 16

Chapter 4: The Comfort Zone...................... 21

Chapter 5: The Lost Vision.........................28

Chapter 6: The Toxic Ripple.......................35

Chapter 7: Self-Fulfilling Prophecy............ 42

Chapter 8: The Wake-Up Call.....................49

Chapter 9: The Turning Point......................56

Chapter 10: The Renewed Flame................ 61

Chapter 11: The Ripple Effect.....................68

Chapter 12: The Legacy.............................75

The Unquenchable Spirit...........................81

Introduction

Leadership, like a flame, can illuminate, inspire, and drive remarkable achievements. But what happens when that flame flickers, dims, and eventually threatens to extinguish? In the demanding and often unforgiving world of leadership, even the most passionate and driven individuals can find their spark waning, their enthusiasm replaced by apathy, and their vision clouded by doubt. This is the insidious journey from inspiration to mediocrity, a path that many leaders, unknowingly or unwillingly, tread.

This book explores the complex and often subtle factors that contribute to the decline of once-inspiring leaders. It delves into the psychological and emotional toll of burnout, the stagnation that comes with complacency, and the disillusionment that arises from a lack of recognition and reward. It examines the toxic ripple effect of demotivated leadership, the self-fulfilling prophecies that perpetuate mediocrity, and the critical wake-up calls that can jolt leaders back to reality.

But this is not a story of despair. It is a story of resilience, reinvention, and the enduring power of the human spirit. It's about recognizing the warning signs, confronting uncomfortable truths, and embracing the journey of self-discovery and transformation. It's about rekindling the flame of passion, reclaiming one's purpose, and leading with renewed vigor and inspiration.

Whether you're a seasoned leader navigating the complexities of your role or an aspiring leader seeking to avoid the pitfalls of mediocrity, this book offers valuable insights and practical guidance. It's a reminder that even the brightest flames can flicker, but with self-awareness, courage, and a commitment to growth, they can be reignited, burning brighter and stronger than ever before.

Join us on this journey as we explore the challenges and triumphs of leadership, the delicate balance between inspiration and mediocrity, and the unyielding spirit that drives us to achieve our full potential.

Why I Wrote This Book

Hello, call me Leo. I've been leading teams in the tech world for over 20 years when this book is being published. Lately, my leadership journey has taken me virtually across the globe, managing teams in places located in Australia, Germany, and all over Canada. It's been quite the adventure, dealing with different time zones and cultures, but it's also given me a unique perspective on leadership.

The idea for this book came from my own experiences over the past years. I've seen firsthand how tough it can be to keep teams motivated and stay inspired when things get rough. Companies cutting costs, team reorganizations, key people leaving, and the slow pace of change in big corporations - it all takes a toll.

I wanted to share what I've learned about navigating these challenges, not just for leaders but for anyone trying to stay motivated and make a difference in their work. It's about finding ways to keep the fire burning, even when storms and hurricanes are passing by.

"This book is for everyone who's been on this crazy ride with me. To the teams I've led, thanks for letting me learn alongside you. To the leaders, bosses and managers who pushed me (even when it was tough), I appreciate the lessons and patience. And most of all, to my family - thanks for always being there, through the highs and the (really) lows ."

Leo

Chapter 1: The Burning Flame

Ever noticed how the brightest flames burn out the quickest?

They say leaders are born, not made. Yeah, okay, maybe there's some truth to that. But here's the thing they forget to mention: that fire in the belly of a truly inspiring leader? The one that makes them go the extra mile, dream big, and get everyone else pumped up too? That fire isn't some magical, everlasting thing. It can flicker, dim, and sometimes... well, it can just go out.

Think about the bosses who've really made a mark on you. The ones who made you believe you could do anything, who pushed you to be your best, who made you actually want to show up to work. These leaders aren't just good at their jobs - they're like walking, talking energy drinks. They've got that special something that sets them apart, and it all starts with a burning flame within.

Fueling the Fire: The 3 Pillars of Inspirational Leadership

First off, these inspiring leaders have a vision. And it's not just some vague idea, it's crystal clear. They know exactly where they're headed, and they can explain it in a way that makes you want to jump on board. They paint this picture of the future that's so awesome, it's almost like you can reach out and touch it. It's this vision that gives their team a sense of purpose, a North Star to guide their efforts. It's what gets people out of bed in the morning, eager to contribute and make a difference. Think of it as the map that guides the ship, ensuring everyone is rowing in the same direction.

But having a vision isn't enough. These leaders are also driven. They're not afraid to get their hands dirty and do the work. They're the first ones in and the last ones out, setting the pace for the entire team. They lead by example, showing everyone else how it's done. Their energy is contagious – you can't help but get caught up in it. When the going gets tough, they're the ones rolling up their sleeves, ready to tackle any obstacle. They inspire others not just with their words, but their actions. They are the engine that propels the ship forward, even against strong currents.

And here's the big one: they actually care about their people. They understand their success depends on the team's success. They invest in their employees, giving them the tools and opportunities they need to grow. They create a culture of trust and respect, where everyone feels valued and heard. They understand that people are their most valuable asset, and they treat them as such. They celebrate their successes, offer support during challenges, and genuinely care about their well-being. They are the heart of the ship, ensuring everyone on board feels valued and supported.

Contagious Glow: The Impact of Inspirational Leadership

When all these things come together, it's magic. Teams with inspiring leaders are more engaged, they get more done, and they come up with the best ideas. They're willing to go above and beyond because they believe in their leader and they're excited about what's coming next. They achieve amazing things, not because they have to, but because they want to. The atmosphere is electric, filled with creativity, collaboration, and a shared sense of purpose. The ship sails smoothly, its crew working in harmony, driven by a shared vision and a sense of belonging.

The Flickering Flame: A Warning

But what happens when that fire starts to die down? When the passion fades, the vision gets blurry, and the drive just isn't there anymore? What happens when those inspiring leaders become... well, just average? That's what we're going to explore next. We'll uncover the subtle signs that even the brightest flames can flicker, setting the stage for a leader's descent into mediocrity. The once-steady ship begins to veer off course, its crew sensing a change in the wind, a shift in the captain's resolve.

Chapter 2: The First Flicker

Think about the last time you started a new job.
Remember that initial excitement? The feeling of endless
possibilities?

Now, fast forward a few years. Maybe the honeymoon phase is over. Maybe you're not bouncing out of bed every morning, eager to tackle the day. Maybe that once-bright flame is starting to flicker a little. It happens to the best of us. And guess what? It happens to leaders too.

Remember those inspiring leaders we talked about? The ones with the clear vision, the relentless drive, and the genuine care for their people? Well, even they can start to lose their spark. It might start small, almost unnoticeable at first. Like a tiny ember losing its glow, the change is subtle but signals a deeper shift. But like a tiny crack in a dam, those little changes can lead to a whole lot of trouble down the line.

The Warning Signs: Recognizing the Shift

One of the first signs that something's off is a change in attitude. That leader who used to be all smiles and positive energy might start to seem a bit... well, grumpy. They might complain more, get frustrated easily, or just seem generally less enthusiastic about their work. It's like their battery is running low, and they just don't have the same zest for life they used to. The once-bright sun begins to dim, casting longer shadows and a cooler light.

Another red flag is a shift in behavior. That leader who used to be proactive and always looking for new challenges might start to become more reactive, just going through the motions. They might avoid taking risks, stick to the safe and familiar, and stop pushing themselves or their team to grow. It's like they're stuck in a rut, and they've lost the motivation to climb out. The once-swift current slows to a trickle, the riverbed becoming visible as the water recedes.

And then there's the dreaded "I don't care" attitude. This one's a real killer. When a leader stops caring about the work, the team, or the bigger picture, it's like a punch to the gut for everyone involved. It creates a toxic atmosphere where people feel undervalued and unappreciated. It's a recipe for disaster, and it can quickly spiral out of control. The once-sturdy foundation begins to crumble, cracks appearing as the structure weakens.

Unmasking the Culprits: Why Leaders Lose Their Spark

So, what causes these once-inspiring leaders to start losing their flame? Well, there are a few common culprits.

Sometimes, it's burnout. The constant pressure to perform, the long hours, the never-ending to-do list – it can all take a toll. Leaders are human too, and they need time to recharge. If they're not taking care of themselves, both physically and mentally, it's only a matter of time before they start to burn out. The flame, once burning bright, has consumed all its fuel, leaving behind only ashes.

Other times, it's a lack of challenge or recognition. If a leader feels like they've hit a plateau, they're not learning and growing anymore, or their efforts aren't being acknowledged through promotions or new opportunities, it's easy to become complacent and unmotivated. They might start to feel like they're just going through the motions, and that their contributions aren't valued. The once-exciting journey has become monotonous, the scenery unchanging, the destination no longer inspiring.

Similarly, inadequate compensation or rewards can also contribute to the first flicker of demotivation. If leaders feel their pay doesn't reflect their efforts or responsibilities, or if they see others being rewarded more generously for less work, it can breed resentment and a sense of unfairness. This can quickly extinguish their passion and drive. The once-generous fire now feels like it's being starved of oxygen, its flames sputtering and struggling to survive.

And there are external factors. Maybe there's been a major setback or disappointment, or maybe the company is going through a tough time. These kinds of challenges can shake even the most confident leader, and it's natural to feel a bit discouraged. The once-calm waters are now choppy, the winds unpredictable, the ship tossed about by forces beyond its control.

In some cases, a demotion can be a particularly devastating blow to a leader's motivation. It can feel like a rejection of their skills and abilities, a sign that they're no longer valued by the organization. This can lead to a profound loss of confidence and a sense of hopelessness, making it even harder to rekindle their passion. The once-proud captain, stripped of their rank and authority, now wanders the deck aimlessly, their spirit broken and their sense of purpose lost.

The Crossroads: A Choice to Make

The first flicker is a crucial juncture. It's a warning sign, a fork in the road. Leaders can choose to ignore it, hoping the flame will rekindle on its own. Or, they can acknowledge it, confront the underlying causes, and take proactive steps to reignite their passion. The ship can continue to drift, hoping the storm will pass, or the captain can take charge, adjust the sails, and navigate towards calmer waters.

The choice is theirs. But the consequences of inaction can be dire. The flicker can turn into a smolder, and eventually, the fire can go out completely, leaving behind only ashes and regret.

In the next chapter, we'll delve deeper into the consequences of ignoring these early warning signs. We'll explore how the slow burn of demotivation can gradually erode a leader's effectiveness, impacting their team, their organization, and ultimately, their own well-being. The once-proud ship, neglected and adrift, begins to take on water, its crew losing hope as the darkness closes in.

Chapter 3: The Slow Burn

Picture this: You're sitting around a campfire, flames dancing, casting a warm glow. It's mesmerizing. But then, life happens - a distraction, a phone call. You look back, and the flames have died down. Just embers now, faintly glowing.

This mirrors the subtle decline of an inspirational leader losing their spark. It's not a sudden explosion, but a slow burn. A gradual fading of the light, a creeping chill replacing the warmth. And before you know it, everything's different. The once vibrant leader is a shadow of their former self.

Remember that proactive, risk-taking leader? The one pushing boundaries, inspiring their team? As motivation dwindles, their leadership style shifts. They become less engaged, risk-averse, focused on just getting by. It's like a once-powerful engine sputtering, struggling to maintain its momentum.

Proactivity turns to reactivity. They're firefighting instead of fire-starting, creating a perpetual crisis mode. The ship's captain, once confidently charting the course, is now merely bailing water, hoping to stay afloat.

Their clear vision blurs. The big picture fades, replaced by day-to-day minutiae. Strategy and innovation give way to maintaining the status quo. The once-bright North Star guiding the team is now obscured by clouds, leaving them disoriented and adrift.

This loss of direction breeds frustration. Team members, once empowered, now feel lost. They question their purpose, their role, their value. The vibrant atmosphere turns to disillusionment. The once-harmonious orchestra is now out of tune, each musician playing their own melody.

Most damaging is the impact on morale. A demotivated leader casts a dark cloud. Their negativity, apathy, lack of enthusiasm - it's contagious. People feel discouraged, undervalued, and uninspired. The once-fertile garden is now parched, plants wilting under the neglect.

This decline impacts productivity. Unmotivated teams don't perform at their best. They're less likely to go the extra mile, innovate, or collaborate. The well-oiled machine grinds to a halt, its gears rusted and unmoving.

Turnover increases. People seek leaders who believe in them, challenge them, inspire them. The best leave, those remaining feel disillusioned. The once-thriving ecosystem collapses, its inhabitants seeking greener pastures.

The Crushing Weight of Unfulfilled Expectations: The Role of Promotions and Rewards

Often, this slow burn is fueled by the absence of promotions or raises. Leaders, like anyone else, crave recognition and advancement. When their hard work and dedication go unnoticed, it's like a slow drip of water on a stone, gradually eroding their motivation and sense of self-worth. The once-ambitious climber, repeatedly denied the chance to ascend higher peaks, begins to question their own abilities and the value of their efforts.

The sting of being passed over for a promotion or seeing others rewarded more generously for less work can be particularly demoralizing. It can create a sense of injustice and resentment, further fueling the flames of demotivation. The once-loyal soldier, seeing their comrades promoted while they remain stagnant, begins to question their allegiance and their commitment to the cause.

In extreme cases, a demotion can be the final blow, shattering a leader's confidence and extinguishing their flame entirely. It's a public declaration of their perceived failure, a stark reminder that they are no longer valued or trusted. The once-proud captain, stripped of their rank and authority, is cast adrift, their compass shattered, their spirit broken.

Delving Deeper: The Psychology of the Slow Burn

This decline isn't just about external factors. It's deeply psychological. Self-esteem erodes, self-efficacy diminishes. The leader's inner fire, their intrinsic motivation, is waning. It's like a pilot losing their love for flying, their once-boundless sky now feeling confining.

This slow burn is insidious. It's not a dramatic fall, but a gradual slide. Recognizing it early is key. The good news? It can be stopped. The flames can be reignited. But it takes courage, self-awareness, and a willingness to change. It's like tending to that dying campfire, carefully adding kindling, gently blowing on the embers, coaxing the flames back to life.

The Breaking Point

In the next chapters, we'll explore why leaders fall into this trap, the warning signs, and the steps to reclaim their passion. Even the best stumble, but it's how they rise that defines them. The phoenix, after all, is reborn from the ashes, stronger and more vibrant than before. But first, it must endure the flames.

Chapter 4: The Comfort Zone

Imagine you're curled up on the couch, wrapped in a warm blanket, binge-watching your favorite show. It feels good, doesn't it? Safe, cozy, no stress.

Now imagine staying there, day after day, week after week. The remote control becomes an extension of your hand, the couch cushions mold to your shape. Sounds tempting, right? But deep down, you know it's not healthy. You're missing out on life, on experiences, on growth. It's like a warm bath - soothing at first, but eventually, the water grows cold and stagnant.

That's the seductive allure of the comfort zone. It's easy, it's familiar, it's... well, comfortable. But for leaders, it's a trap. A slow, insidious trap that can lead to stagnation, mediocrity, and ultimately, the death of their inspiration. It's the siren song that lures sailors to their doom, promising peace but delivering only oblivion.

The Siren's Call: The Allure of Complacency

Remember those once-inspiring leaders we've been talking about? The ones who burned bright with passion, vision, and drive? Well, as they settle into their comfort zone, that fire starts to dim. They become less willing to take risks, less eager to learn and grow, and more focused on just maintaining the status quo. The once-blazing bonfire dwindles to a few flickering embers, its warmth and light fading into the encroaching darkness.

It's like they've climbed a mountain, reached the summit, and decided to just stay there. The view is nice, sure. But they're missing out on all the other mountains out there, all the other challenges and adventures waiting to be discovered. They've reached a plateau, a comfortable resting place, but the true summit, the one that represents their full potential, remains tantalizingly out of reach.

The Price of Comfort: The Perils of Stagnation

The comfort zone is a dangerous place for leaders because it breeds complacency. When you're not pushing yourself, not challenging yourself, not stepping outside your comfort zone, you stop growing. You become stagnant, stuck in a rut, and that's a recipe for disaster. It's like a plant that's stopped reaching for the sunlight, its leaves turning yellow and its roots withering away.

Think about it this way: a muscle that's not used will atrophy. It will weaken, shrink, and eventually become useless. The same is true for our minds, our skills, and our leadership abilities. If we're not constantly challenging ourselves, pushing ourselves to learn and grow, we'll start to decline. The once-sharp sword, left unused, becomes dull and rusty, its edge no longer capable of cutting through the challenges that lie ahead.

And that decline can be subtle at first. It might start with a few missed opportunities, a few projects that don't quite meet their potential. But over time, it becomes more and more noticeable. The leader's decision-making becomes less sharp, their problem-solving skills become less effective, and their ability to inspire and motivate their team diminishes. The once-powerful engine starts to misfire, its performance sluggish and unreliable.

The comfort zone can also lead to a lack of innovation. When leaders are afraid to take risks, they're less likely to come up with new ideas, to experiment, to try new things. They stick to the tried and true, the safe and familiar, and that can stifle creativity and growth for the entire team. The once-fertile ground becomes barren, its potential for growth stifled by the lack of fresh ideas and bold initiatives.

The Toll on Well-being: The Personal Cost of Complacency

And let's not forget the impact on the leader's own well-being. When you're stuck in a rut, it's easy to become bored, frustrated, and even depressed. You lose that sense of excitement, that passion that used to drive you. And that can have a ripple effect on every aspect of your life. The once-vibrant individual becomes a hollow shell, their spirit dimmed by the lack of challenge and fulfillment.

Breaking Free: The Path to Renewed Growth

So, how do leaders break free from the comfort zone? It starts with recognizing the trap and being willing to step outside of it. It means embracing challenges, seeking out new experiences, and constantly pushing yourself to learn and grow. It's time to leave the safety of the harbor, to unfurl the sails, and to set out on a new adventure.

It means being willing to fail, to make mistakes, and to learn from them. It means being open to new ideas, even if they challenge your existing beliefs. It means being uncomfortable, at least some of the time. It's about embracing the storm, navigating the waves, and emerging stronger and more resilient on the other side.

Because the truth is, growth doesn't happen in the comfort zone. It happens on the other side of fear, on the edge of uncertainty. It happens when we're willing to step outside of our comfort zone and embrace the unknown. It's in the uncharted territories, the unexplored landscapes, that we discover our true potential.

From Comfort to Conquest: A Call to Action

So, if you're a leader, or you aspire to be one, don't let the comfort zone lure you in. Embrace the challenges, seek out new experiences, and never stop growing. Because the world needs your passion, your vision, and your drive. And the only way to keep those flames burning bright is to keep pushing yourself, keep learning, and keep stepping outside of your comfort zone. It's time to trade the familiar for the extraordinary, the safe for the exhilarating, the mediocre for the exceptional.

But what happens when leaders fail to heed this call, when they remain trapped in their comfort zone? In the next chapter, we will explore the insidious consequences of complacency, the gradual erosion of a leader's effectiveness, and the devastating impact it can have on their team and their organization. The ship, once a symbol of hope and progress, now lies stranded on the rocks, its crew disheartened and its future uncertain.

Chapter 5: The Lost Vision

Imagine going on a road trip without a map or GPS. You know you want to go somewhere, but you're not exactly sure where. You just start driving, hoping you'll figure it out along the way.

Sounds like a recipe for disaster, right? You'll probably end up lost, frustrated, and wondering why you even bothered in the first place. Well, that's precisely what happens to leaders who lose their vision. They start out with a clear destination in mind, but somewhere along the way, they get sidetracked. They lose their focus, their sense of purpose, and they end up wandering aimlessly. It's like a once-bright lighthouse, its beam now extinguished, leaving ships to navigate the treacherous waters without guidance.

From Clarity to Confusion: The Fading of the North Star

Remember those inspiring leaders we talked about in the first chapter? The ones with the crystal-clear vision of the future? Well, as they become demotivated, that vision starts to fade. It becomes blurry, distant, and eventually, it disappears altogether. The once-vivid picture of the future, painted in bold strokes, now fades to a pale watercolor, its details lost in a haze of uncertainty.

It's like they're driving in a fog, unable to see more than a few feet in front of them. They're just reacting to whatever comes their way, instead of proactively charting their course. They're lost, and they don't even know it. The compass needle spins wildly, pointing in every direction but the right one.

The Blueprint Lost: The Impact on Decision-Making and Strategy

This loss of vision can have a devastating impact on a leader's effectiveness. Without a clear destination in mind, it's impossible to make sound decisions, to prioritize effectively, or to inspire and motivate their team. The ship, once sailing confidently towards a known port, now drifts aimlessly, its crew unsure of their purpose or their ultimate goal.

Think about it this way: if you're building a house, you need a blueprint. You need to know what you're building, how it's going to look, and how all the pieces fit together. Without that blueprint, you're just stacking bricks on top of each other, hoping for the best. The architect's vision, once meticulously detailed, now lies crumpled and forgotten, leaving the builders to improvise and guess their way through the project.

The same is true for leadership. Without a clear vision, leaders are just reacting to the day-to-day challenges, putting out fires, and hoping they're moving in the right direction. But they're not. They're just spinning their wheels, wasting time and energy, and ultimately, failing to achieve their full potential. The once-grand symphony is now a cacophony of dissonant notes, each musician playing their own tune without a conductor to guide them.

The Domino Effect: The Impact on Team Morale and Cohesion

This lack of vision can also have a demoralizing effect on the team. When people don't know where they're headed, or why they're doing what they're doing, it's hard to stay motivated and engaged. They start to question the purpose of their work, and they lose that sense of shared goal that used to unite them. The once-united army, marching towards a common objective, now splinters into factions, each unsure of their role in the larger battle.

And without that shared goal, it's hard to build a cohesive, high-performing team. People start to pull in different directions, pursuing their own agendas instead of working together towards a common objective. The result is a fragmented, disjointed team that's unable to achieve its full potential. The once-powerful engine, its cylinders misfiring, struggles to propel the vehicle forward.

Reclaiming the Vision: The Path to Renewed Purpose

So, how do leaders reclaim their lost vision? It starts with introspection and self-reflection. They need to take a step back, look at the big picture, and ask themselves some tough questions:

- What do I really want to achieve?

- What impact do I want to make on the world?

- What legacy do I want to leave behind?

Once they have a clearer sense of their purpose, they can start to develop a new vision for the future. This vision should be inspiring, challenging, and something that everyone on the team can rally around. It's time to redraw the map, to plot a new course, and to set sail towards a brighter horizon.

Sharing the Vision: Inspiring and Empowering the Team

It's also important for leaders to communicate their vision clearly and consistently. They need to paint a picture of the future that's so compelling, it makes people want to jump on board. They must share their passion, enthusiasm and belief in the possibilities. The lighthouse keeper must relight the beacon, its beam cutting through the fog and guiding the lost ships back to safety.

And finally, leaders must empower their team to help them achieve that vision. They must give people the autonomy, resources and support they need to achieve it. They need to create a culture of trust and collaboration, where everyone feels like they're part of something bigger than themselves. The captain must rally the crew, reminding them of their shared purpose and inspiring them to work together towards a common goal.

From Lost to Found: The Power of a Renewed Vision

Because when leaders have a clear vision, and they can inspire their team to share that vision, anything is possible. They can achieve amazing things, overcome any obstacle, and leave a lasting legacy. The ship, once adrift, now sails confidently towards its destination, its crew energized and united.

But what happens when leaders fail to reclaim their lost vision? When they keep wandering aimlessly, with no clear sense of purpose or direction? In the next chapter, we will explore the devastating consequences of this lack of vision, the toxic ripple effect it creates, and the urgent need for leaders to find their way back to the light. The ship, lost at sea, sends out a distress signal, its crew hoping for rescue before it's too late.

Chapter 6: The Toxic Ripple

Imagine a pebble tossed into a still pond. The ripples spread outward, disturbing the tranquility, affecting everything in their path. A single act, a seemingly insignificant disturbance, can have far-reaching consequences.

This is precisely what happens when a leader becomes demotivated. Their negativity, apathy, and lack of inspiration create a toxic ripple effect that spreads throughout the team and the entire organization. It's like a virus, silently infecting everyone it touches, leaving a trail of disengagement, low morale, and declining performance in its wake. The once-pristine pond, teeming with life, now stagnates, its surface marred by a spreading film of toxicity.

The Transformation: From Beacon to Shadow

The once-inspiring leader, who used to be a beacon of positivity, radiating energy and enthusiasm, now casts a long, dark shadow. Their passion, once contagious and uplifting, has been replaced by a disheartening aura of indifference. The once-bright star, a guiding light in the night sky, now flickers and dims, its brilliance fading into obscurity.

This transformation is not sudden, but gradual erosion. The once-proactive leader, always seeking new challenges and pushing boundaries, now hesitates, avoids risks, and settles for mediocrity. Their once-clear vision, which used to guide their every decision and inspire their team, has become blurred and distant. They're no longer steering the ship, but rather drifting aimlessly, reacting to whatever comes their way. The once-mighty oak, its branches reaching towards the heavens, now stands withered and gnarled, its leaves turning brown and falling to the ground.

The Spreading Unease: A Climate of Uncertainty

This lack of direction and purpose creates a sense of unease and uncertainty within the team. Employees, who once felt empowered and motivated, now feel lost and confused. They start to question the meaning of their work, their role within the organization, and their own value. The once-collaborative and vibrant atmosphere is replaced by a sense of disillusionment and apathy. The once-harmonious choir, singing in unison, now falters, each voice hesitant and uncertain, their melody disjointed and discordant.

The Contagion of Negativity: A Blight on Morale

The demotivated leader's negativity further exacerbates the situation. Their complaints, criticisms, and focus on problems rather than solutions create a toxic environment where optimism and enthusiasm struggle to survive. Their pessimism seeps into every conversation, every meeting, every interaction, casting a dark cloud over the entire team. The once-clear stream, its waters sparkling in the sunlight, now flows sluggishly, polluted by the toxins that seep from its banks.

Unfair Treatment: Fueling the Flames of Resentment

This toxic atmosphere is often intensified by perceived unfairness in the workplace. When deserving employees are repeatedly passed over for promotions or raises, it breeds resentment and a sense of injustice. Witnessing colleagues receive recognition and rewards for seemingly lesser contributions can be a bitter pill to swallow, further eroding morale and fueling the flames of demotivation. The once-balanced scales now tip heavily to one side, their imbalance a constant reminder of the perceived inequity.

The Vicious Cycle: A Self-Perpetuating Downward Spiral

Perhaps the most insidious aspect of this toxic ripple effect is its self-perpetuating nature. The leader's demotivation feeds the team's disengagement, which in turn reinforces the leader's negativity. It's a vicious cycle that, if left unchecked, can spiral out of control, leading to a complete breakdown of trust, communication, and productivity. The once-healthy ecosystem, teeming with life, now teeters on the brink of collapse, its delicate balance disrupted by a cascade of negative feedback loops.

The Fallout: Far-Reaching Consequences

The consequences of this downward spiral are far-reaching. Talented employees, seeking a more positive and fulfilling work environment, start to leave. Those who remain become increasingly disengaged, their performance suffering as a result. The organization's overall productivity declines, innovation stagnates, and its reputation suffers. The once-thriving city, its streets bustling with activity, now stands deserted, its buildings crumbling, its spirit broken.

Moreover, the impact of a demotivated leader extends beyond the workplace. Their negativity and apathy can seep into their personal lives, affecting their relationships with family and friends. The once vibrant and fulfilled individual becomes withdrawn and joyless, their overall well-being compromised. The once-radiant sun, its light dimmed by a passing cloud, struggles to warm the earth below.

The Call to Action: Recognizing and Addressing the Toxicity

Recognizing the signs of demotivation in leaders is crucial for preventing the spread of this toxic ripple effect. It requires a keen eye for subtle changes in behavior, attitude, and communication. It also demands a willingness to address the underlying issues, whether they stem from burnout, lack of challenge, perceived unfairness, or personal struggles. It's time to sound the alarm, to raise the red flag, and to take decisive action to contain the spreading contagion.

By proactively addressing these issues, leaders can reignite their passion, reclaim their purpose, and break free from the cycle of negativity. They can transform their leadership style, inspire their teams, and create a positive and productive work environment where everyone can thrive. It's time to restore the balance, to cleanse the waters, and to breathe new life into the dying ecosystem.

The Turning Point

In the following chapters, we will delve deeper into the strategies and techniques that leaders can employ to overcome demotivation and reclaim their role as beacons of inspiration. We will explore the importance of self-reflection, continuous learning, and seeking support from mentors and coaches. We will also examine the power of setting new goals, embracing challenges, and celebrating successes, both big and small. The phoenix, rising from the ashes, spreads its wings and takes flight, its fiery rebirth a symbol of hope and renewal.

Chapter 7: Self-Fulfilling Prophecy

Ever heard the saying, "Whether you think you can or you think you can't, you're right?"

It's a simple statement, but it packs a powerful punch. And it's especially true when it comes to leadership. When a leader starts to believe they're no longer capable, no longer inspiring, no longer effective, it becomes a self-fulfilling prophecy. Their negative mindset and behaviors create a downward spiral that's hard to escape. It's like a dark cloud forming overhead, casting a shadow of doubt and negativity that grows larger with each passing day.

The Seeds of Doubt: Nurturing a Negative Mindset

Think back to those early signs of demotivation we talked about in Chapter 2. The grumpiness, the lack of enthusiasm, the avoidance of risk. These are all symptoms of a leader who's starting to doubt themselves, to question their abilities, and to lose faith in their vision. The once-confident captain now hesitates, their hand trembling on the ship's wheel, their eyes scanning the horizon for signs of danger.

Several factors can contribute to this growing sense of self-doubt. The absence of recognition or reward can chip away at a leader's confidence. When their hard work and dedication go unnoticed, or when they see others being promoted or receiving raises while they remain stagnant, it can plant seeds of doubt in their minds. The once-bright flame of ambition flickers as the leader questions their worth and the value of their contributions.

Similarly, the sting of a demotion can be a devastating blow to a leader's self-belief. It can feel like a public declaration of their perceived failure, a rejection of their skills and abilities. This can lead to a profound sense of inadequacy and a reluctance to take risks or assert their authority. The once-proud lion, wounded and scarred, retreats to the shadows, their roar silenced by the echoes of their perceived defeat.

The Toxic Cycle: Reinforcing Negative Beliefs

As these doubts grow, they start to affect the leader's behavior. They become less confident, less decisive, and less willing to take risks. They start to micromanage their team, second-guessing every decision and stifling creativity. They become less approachable, less open to feedback, and more likely to shut down any dissenting opinions. The once-open door to the captain's quarters is now firmly closed, the windows shuttered, the leader isolated and withdrawn.

This creates a toxic environment where people feel like they can't do anything right. They're afraid to speak up, to share their ideas, or to take initiative. They become disengaged, demotivated, and ultimately, less productive. The once-vibrant crew, full of energy and enthusiasm, now moves about the ship like listless ghosts, their spirits dampened by the captain's negativity.

And the worst part is, the leader's negative mindset reinforces their own beliefs. They see their team's lack of enthusiasm and productivity as proof that they're right, that they're not good enough, that they're failing. The captain, seeing the crew's disengagement, interprets it as a confirmation of their own inadequacy, further fueling their self-doubt.

It's a vicious cycle, a self-fulfilling prophecy that can be incredibly difficult to break. But it's not impossible. The key is to recognize the pattern and take proactive steps to change it. It's time to break the spell, to dispel the dark cloud, and to reclaim the light of positivity and self-belief.

Breaking Free: The Path to Self-Empowerment

It starts with self-awareness. Leaders must be honest with themselves about their thoughts and feelings. They need to acknowledge their doubts and fears, and they need to be willing to challenge their negative beliefs. It's time to open the captain's quarters, to let in the fresh air and sunlight, and to confront the demons that lurk within.

It's also important to seek out support. Talk to a trusted friend, a mentor, or a coach. Get feedback from your team. Sometimes, all it takes is an outside perspective to help you see things in a new light. The crew, sensing their captain's distress, offers their support, their loyalty, and their unwavering belief in their leader's ability to navigate the storm.

And finally, it's about taking action. Don't let your negative thoughts and feelings paralyze you. Set small, achievable goals, and celebrate your successes. Focus on the positive, and remind yourself of all the things you've accomplished in the past. It's time to hoist the sails, to adjust the course, and to set out on a new journey, fueled by renewed confidence and determination.

The Journey Continues: Overcoming Challenges and Embracing Growth

Remember, leadership is a journey, not a destination. There will be setbacks, challenges, and moments of doubt. But the truly great leaders are the ones who can overcome those challenges, learn from their mistakes, and keep moving forward. The ship may encounter rough seas, but with a captain who believes in themselves and their crew, it will weather the storm and emerge stronger than ever.

So, if you're a leader who's caught in the trap of a self-fulfilling prophecy, don't give up. Break the cycle. Challenge your negative beliefs, seek out support, and take action. You're capable of more than you think. You're capable of inspiring, motivating, and leading your team to greatness. The flame may have flickered, but it's not extinguished. With care and attention, it can be rekindled, burning brighter and stronger than before.

Believe in yourself, and others will believe in you too.

The Turning Point

But how does a leader break free from this self-destructive cycle? How do they shift their mindset, reclaim their confidence, and reignite their passion? In the next chapter, we'll explore the pivotal moments that can trigger a leader's awakening, the wake-up calls that jolt them out of their complacency and set them on a path towards transformation and renewal. The storm clouds may be gathering, but on the horizon, a glimmer of hope appears, a beacon signaling the possibility of a new beginning.

Chapter 8: The Wake-Up Call

Imagine sleepwalking through life, oblivious to the world around you. Then, suddenly, a loud crash jolts you awake. You're disoriented, confused, but also undeniably alert.

This is the experience many leaders have when they finally realize they've fallen into the trap of mediocrity. It's a wake-up call, a moment of clarity that shakes them out of their complacency and forces them to confront the reality of their situation. It's like a sudden splash of cold water, shocking the system and bringing a sense of urgency and awareness.

The Rude Awakening: Recognizing the Decline

These wake-up calls can come in many forms. It might be a scathing performance review, a missed promotion, or a sudden realization that their team is disengaged and uninspired. It might be a personal crisis, a health scare, or a major life event that forces them to re-evaluate their priorities. The alarm clock blares, the mirror reflects a haggard face, the calendar shows missed deadlines and unfulfilled promises.

The Sting of Stagnation: The Impact of Lack of Recognition

In many cases, the wake-up call comes in the form of unfulfilled expectations. It's the sting of being passed over for a promotion, the disappointment of a stagnant salary, or the realization that their hard work and dedication are going unnoticed and unrewarded. The once-promising career path now seems to have hit a dead end, the ladder to success feeling increasingly out of reach.

This lack of recognition can be a particularly bitter pill to swallow for leaders who have poured their heart and soul into their work. It can lead to feelings of resentment, frustration, and a sense of being undervalued. The once-motivated employee, their efforts seemingly overlooked, begins to question their worth and their commitment to the organization.

In some cases, the wake-up call can be even more jarring, taking the form of a demotion. This can be a devastating blow to a leader's confidence and self-worth, signaling a loss of trust and a perceived failure to meet expectations. The once-proud captain, stripped of their rank and authority, is forced to confront the harsh reality of their perceived shortcomings.

Whatever the trigger, it's a moment of reckoning. The leader is forced to confront the consequences of their demotivation, the damage they've done to their team, and the missed opportunities that have slipped through their fingers. The once-clear path now reveals itself as a dead end, the once-bright future now shrouded in doubt and uncertainty.

It's a painful realization, but it's also a necessary one. Because without that wake-up call, the leader might continue sleepwalking through life, oblivious to the damage they're causing and the potential they're wasting. The sleepwalker stumbles, their eyes finally open to the precipice they've been unknowingly approaching.

The Turning Point: A Choice to Make

The wake-up call is a turning point, a chance for the leader to take stock of their situation and make a change. It's an opportunity to break free from the cycle of negativity, to reclaim their passion and purpose, and to become the leader they were meant to be. The crossroads appear, one path leading back to the familiar comfort of mediocrity, the other towards the uncharted territory of growth and renewal.

But it's not an easy process. It takes courage, self-awareness, and a willingness to confront some uncomfortable truths. It means admitting that you've lost your way, that you've let yourself down, and that you've let your team down. It's time to face the mirror, to acknowledge the cracks in the facade, and to accept responsibility for the journey that led to this point.

It also means being willing to change. To let go of old habits, to embrace new challenges, and to step outside of your comfort zone. It means being open to feedback, even if it's painful to hear. It's time to shed the old skin, to embrace the discomfort of growth, and to emerge transformed.

The Gift of a Fresh Start: Embracing the Opportunity

But the rewards are worth it. When a leader heeds the wake-up call, they can experience a profound transformation. They can rediscover their passion, vision and drive. They can rebuild their team, reignite their enthusiasm, and achieve extraordinary results. The phoenix rises from the ashes, its wings ablaze with a renewed fire, ready to soar to new heights.

The wake-up call is a gift, a chance for a fresh start. It's an opportunity to learn from your mistakes, to grow as a leader, and to create a legacy that you can be proud of. The caterpillar, after a period of darkness and transformation, emerges as a beautiful butterfly, ready to embrace a new world of possibilities.

The Call to Action: Heeding the Alarm

So, if you're a leader who's feeling stuck, uninspired, or just plain lost, pay attention to the signs. Listen to your gut, be honest with yourself, and don't be afraid to ask for help. The alarm bells are ringing, the warning lights are flashing - it's time to wake up and take action.

Because the wake-up call might be just what you need to shake things up, to get back on track, and to become the best leader you can be. The journey to rediscovering your passion and purpose may be challenging, but the destination is worth the effort.

Embarking on the Journey of Reinvention

In the next chapter, we'll explore the journey of self-discovery and reinvention that leaders embark on after heeding the wake-up call. We'll delve into the strategies and practices they can employ to reignite their passion, reclaim their purpose, and emerge as the inspirational leaders they were meant to be. The compass needle steadies, pointing towards a new horizon, as the ship sets sail on a voyage of transformation and renewal.

Chapter 9: The Turning Point

Imagine standing at a crossroads, one path leading back to the familiar, comfortable mediocrity, the other shrouded in mist, promising growth but demanding courage.

This is the pivotal moment for leaders who've heard the wake-up call. Recognizing their demotivation and its consequences, they face a choice: continue the downward spiral, or embark on a journey of reinvention. It's the hero's moment of truth, the call to adventure that beckons them to leave their ordinary world and step into the unknown.

The Courage to Change: Embracing the Unknown

Choosing the path of reinvention isn't easy. It demands courage, resilience, a willingness to step outside the familiar. It means facing fears, overcoming obstacles, embracing the unknown. It's like stepping off a cliff, trusting that wings will sprout before you hit the ground. But for those who take the leap, the rewards are immeasurable.

Self-Reflection: The Journey Inward

Reinvention begins with introspection. Leaders must delve into their motivations, values, aspirations. It's time for tough questions:

- What truly inspires me? *What makes my heart sing, my mind race with possibilities?*

- What are my strengths and weaknesses? *Where do I excel, and where do I need to grow?*

- What impact do I want to make? *What mark do I want to leave on the world?*

This self-discovery can be uncomfortable. It's confronting shortcomings, acknowledging mistakes, letting go of outdated beliefs. It's like cleaning out a cluttered attic, discarding the useless and rediscovering forgotten treasures.

But it's also liberating. Understanding oneself uncovers the roots of demotivation, enabling strategies to overcome it. Passions, strengths, unique values - all are rediscovered. It's like polishing a tarnished mirror, revealing the true reflection beneath.

Setting a New Course: From Vision to Action

With clarity comes the power to set new goals, to chart a course towards them. This might mean seeking challenges, learning new skills, and building relationships. It's time to draw a new map, one that leads to unexplored territories, to hidden treasures waiting to be unearthed.

Patience and persistence are key. Change takes time, setbacks are inevitable. But by focusing on goals, celebrating small wins, momentum builds. It's like planting a seed, nurturing it with care, watching it slowly but surely sprout and grow.

Seeking Guidance: The Power of Support

Mentors, coaches, trusted colleagues - their support is invaluable. They offer guidance, encouragement, accountability, helping leaders stay on track. It's like having a seasoned guide on a treacherous mountain climb, their experience and wisdom lighting the way.

Transformation: The Emergence of the New Leader

The turning point is a metamorphosis. Leaders shed their old skin, emerging as their best selves. Passion, purpose, inspiration reignited. The caterpillar, after a period of darkness and introspection, emerges as a vibrant butterfly, ready to take flight.

By embracing challenges, facing fears, committing to growth, leaders create a ripple effect. They transform their teams, their organizations, their communities. The once-dimmed light now shines brightly, casting its glow far and wide, inspiring others to follow its path.

A Call to Action: Embrace the Turning Point

If you're ready to step out of the shadows and into the light, embrace the turning point. It's a journey of self-discovery, reinvention, and ultimately, fulfillment. The crossroads await. Choose the path less traveled, the one that leads to growth, purpose, and a legacy that will endure.

But what happens when a leader successfully navigates this turning point? How does their renewed passion and purpose impact their team, their organization, and the world around them? In the next chapter, we'll explore the ripple effect of this transformation, the positive contagion that spreads outward, inspiring others to reach their full potential. The flame, once flickering, now burns brightly, casting its warmth and light on all who gather around it.

Chapter 10: The Renewed Flame

Picture a phoenix rising from the ashes, its wings ablaze with a renewed fire. It's a symbol of rebirth, transformation, overcoming adversity and emerging stronger than ever before.

This is the image of a leader who has successfully navigated the turning point, who has emerged from the depths of demotivation and reclaimed their passion and purpose. They are no longer a shadow of their former self, but a beacon of inspiration, radiating energy, enthusiasm, and a renewed sense of purpose. The once-dimmed light now shines brightly, casting its glow far and wide, illuminating the path for others to follow.

Transformation Unveiled: The Leader Reborn

The transformation is evident in every aspect of their leadership. Their once-dimmed vision now shines brightly, guiding their every decision and inspiring their team. Their once-hesitant and risk-averse approach has been replaced by a bold and innovative spirit, eager to embrace new challenges and explore uncharted territories. The once-dormant volcano now erupts with renewed vigor, its lava flows carving new paths and creating fertile ground for growth.

Their communication is clear, concise, and infused with a contagious enthusiasm. They articulate their vision with passion, painting a vivid picture of the future that motivates and empowers their team. They actively listen to their employees, valuing their input and fostering a culture of collaboration and open communication. The once-silent symphony now resonates with a powerful melody, each instrument playing in harmony, their music inspiring and uplifting.

The Contagion of Inspiration: Igniting the Team

The renewed flame also ignites a transformation in their team. The once-disengaged and unmotivated employees now feel energized and inspired. They are eager to contribute, innovate and exceed expectations. The workplace is abuzz with creativity, collaboration, and a shared sense of purpose. The once-barren landscape now blooms with vibrant colors, each flower reaching for the sun, its petals unfurling in a celebration of life.

The leader's renewed passion also has a profound impact on their own well-being. They are no longer burdened by the weight of negativity and apathy. Instead, they exude confidence, optimism, and a zest for life. Their work is no longer a chore, but a source of fulfillment and joy. The once-weary traveler now strides confidently towards the horizon, their steps light and their spirit renewed.

Nurturing the Flame: Sustaining the Transformation

This transformation is not a one-time event, but rather an ongoing process. The renewed flame requires constant nurturing and attention. Leaders must remain committed to their personal and professional growth, seeking out new challenges, learning new skills, and continuously expanding their horizons. The phoenix, having risen from the ashes, must continue to soar, its wings ever-stronger, its spirit ever-bright.

They must also be mindful of the potential triggers for demotivation, such as burnout, lack of challenge, or personal struggles. By recognizing these early warning signs and taking proactive steps to address them, they can ensure that their flame continues to burn brightly. The gardener, having revived the wilting plants, must continue to tend to them, providing water, sunlight, and nourishment to ensure their continued growth.

A Testament to Resilience: The Power of Renewal

The renewed flame is a testament to the resilience of the human spirit, the power of self-reflection, and the transformative potential of leadership. It is a reminder that even in the darkest of times, there is always hope for a brighter future. The once-dormant volcano, now awakened, reminds us that even the most seemingly lifeless landscapes can be transformed by the forces of nature.

By sharing their stories of reinvention and triumph, these leaders inspire others to embark on their own journeys of self-discovery and growth. They demonstrate that it is never too late to reclaim one's passion, to reignite one's purpose, and to make a positive impact on the world. The phoenix, soaring through the sky, leaves a trail of hope and inspiration in its wake.

Beyond Personal Growth: A Catalyst for Organizational Success

The renewed flame is not just a symbol of personal transformation, but also a catalyst for organizational success.

It creates a ripple effect of positivity, engagement, and high performance that permeates every aspect of the company culture. The revitalized ecosystem thrives, its inhabitants flourishing, its energy radiating outward.

A Call to Embrace the Journey: The Enduring Legacy

So, if you're a leader who has experienced the darkness of demotivation, take heart. The path to renewal is within your reach. Embrace the challenges, seek out support, and never give up on your dreams. The journey may be long and arduous, but the destination is a life filled with passion, purpose, and the opportunity to make a lasting impact.

Remember, the phoenix rises from the ashes, stronger and more vibrant than ever before. And so can you.

But the journey doesn't end with personal transformation. The renewed flame of a leader has the power to ignite a chain reaction, inspiring and empowering others to reach their full potential. In the next chapter, we will explore the ripple effect of this renewed inspiration, the positive contagion that spreads outward, transforming teams, organizations, and even communities. The beacon, once extinguished, now shines brightly, guiding countless ships towards a safe harbor.

Chapter 11: The Ripple Effect

Think of a single drop of water falling into a calm pool. It creates ripples that spread outward, touching every corner of the surface. A small action, a seemingly insignificant disturbance, can set in motion a chain reaction of profound change.

This is what happens when a leader's renewed flame shines brightly. Their revitalized passion, purpose, and drive create a positive ripple effect that touches every member of their team and extends throughout the entire organization. It's a contagious energy, an infectious enthusiasm that transforms the workplace and inspires everyone to reach their full potential. The once-still waters now come alive with movement, each ripple carrying the energy of the initial drop, spreading its influence far and wide.

From Disengagement to Empowerment: The Team's Transformation

The once-disengaged and demotivated team members now feel a renewed sense of purpose and excitement. They are drawn to the leader's positive energy, their clear vision, and their unwavering commitment to success. They feel valued, appreciated, and empowered to contribute their best work. The once-scattered flock of birds now takes flight, soaring in unison, their wings catching the wind and carrying them towards a shared destination.

The workplace, once stagnant and lackluster, is now abuzz with activity. Collaboration flourishes, innovation thrives, and productivity soars. Employees are no longer just going through the motions, but actively seeking out new challenges and opportunities for growth. The once-quiet forest now resonates with the sounds of life, each creature playing its part in the vibrant symphony of nature.

Building Trust and Respect: A Culture of Collaboration

The leader's renewed flame also fosters a culture of trust and respect. Open communication is encouraged, feedback is welcomed, and everyone feels comfortable sharing their ideas and perspectives. This creates a safe and supportive environment where individuals can thrive and the team can achieve extraordinary results. The once-barren soil now nurtures a thriving garden, each plant supported and nourished, its roots intertwining to create a strong and resilient foundation.

Beyond the Team: A Wider Impact

The ripple effect extends beyond the immediate team, influencing other departments and even external stakeholders. The organization's reputation improves, attracting top talent and fostering strong partnerships. The company becomes known for its positive culture, its innovative spirit, and its commitment to excellence. The once-isolated island now becomes a bustling hub of activity, its shores welcoming visitors from far and wide, its influence spreading across the vast ocean.

Personal and Professional Growth: The Leader's Evolution

The leader's renewed passion also has a profound impact on their own personal and professional growth. They become more confident, more resilient, and more effective in their role. They are no longer afraid to take risks, to challenge the status quo, and to push the boundaries of what is possible. The once-hesitant hiker now strides confidently along the mountain path, their eyes fixed on the summit, their spirit undaunted by the challenges ahead.

This newfound confidence and clarity also translates into their personal lives. They are more present, more engaged, and more fulfilled in their relationships with family and friends. Their overall well-being improves, and they radiate a sense of joy and contentment that is contagious to those around them. The once-dimmed light now shines brightly, not only illuminating their own path but also casting a warm glow on those they encounter along the way.

The Power of Positive Influence: A Testament to Leadership

The ripple effect of a leader's renewed flame is a testament to the power of positive influence. It demonstrates that one person's passion and purpose can have a transformative impact on an entire organization and beyond. The single drop of water, falling into the calm pool, has created a symphony of ripples, each one carrying the potential for growth, change, and renewal.

Inspiring Others: A Chain Reaction of Growth

By sharing their stories of reinvention and triumph, these leaders inspire others to embrace their own potential for growth and change. They demonstrate that it is never too late to reclaim one's passion, to reignite one's purpose, and to make a positive difference in the world. The phoenix, rising from the ashes, ignites a chain reaction of hope and transformation, inspiring others to spread their wings and soar.

The True Essence of Leadership: Empowering Others to Thrive

The ripple effect is a reminder that leadership is not just about achieving results, but also about inspiring others to achieve their best. It's about creating a culture of positivity, collaboration, and continuous improvement where everyone can thrive. The leader, like a skilled conductor, guides the orchestra, each musician playing their part in creating a masterpiece of sound.

A Call to Embrace the Ripple: Spreading the Light

So, if you're a leader who has rediscovered your flame, embrace the ripple effect. Share your passion, your vision, and your enthusiasm with those around you. Inspire others to reach their full potential, and together, create a wave of positive change that transforms your organization and the world. Let your light shine brightly, casting its warmth and radiance on all who cross your path. For in the end, it is the collective glow of countless flames that illuminates the world and guides us towards a brighter future.

But the ripple effect doesn't stop there. The impact of a leader's renewed inspiration can extend far beyond their immediate sphere of influence, leaving a lasting legacy that continues to shape the world long after they are gone. In the next chapter, we will explore the enduring legacy of inspirational leaders, the mark they leave on their teams, their organizations, and the world at large. The ripples, once confined to the pool, now flow into the river, carrying their transformative power to distant shores.

Chapter 12: The Legacy

Think of the leaders who have left an indelible mark on history. The ones whose names are synonymous with innovation, courage, and unwavering commitment to their vision. Figures like Martin Luther King Jr., Mahatma Gandhi, or Steve Jobs.

These are the leaders who have not only achieved great things, but have also inspired countless others to follow in their footsteps. They have left behind a legacy that transcends their own accomplishments, a legacy that continues to shape the world long after they are gone. Their footprints are etched in the sands of time, their echoes reverberating through the corridors of history.

Beyond Accomplishments: The Mark of a True Leader

This is the ultimate goal of every leader: to create a lasting impact, to leave the world a better place than they found it. And for those who have overcome the challenges of demotivation and reclaimed their passion, this legacy is built on a foundation of resilience, perseverance, and a deep commitment to personal and professional growth. It's not just about reaching the summit, but about paving the path for others to follow.

Their stories serve as a beacon of hope for others, demonstrating that it is never too late to reignite one's purpose, to rediscover one's passion, and to make a meaningful contribution to the world. They inspire others to embrace their own potential for greatness, to overcome obstacles, and to pursue their dreams with unwavering determination. They are the living proof that the human spirit can triumph over adversity, that the flame of inspiration can be rekindled, no matter how dim it may have become.

Mentorship and Empowerment: Nurturing the Next Generation

The legacy of these leaders is not just about their individual achievements, but also about the impact they have had on those around them. They have mentored and empowered countless individuals, helping them develop their own leadership skills and to achieve their own goals. They have created a culture of innovation, collaboration, and continuous improvement that continues to thrive long after they have moved on. They are the master craftsmen, passing on their skills and knowledge to their apprentices, ensuring that their craft endures for generations to come.

Their legacy is also reflected in the organizations they have built or transformed. These organizations are known for their strong values, their commitment to excellence, and their unwavering focus on making a positive impact on the world. They are places where people are proud to work, where they feel valued and supported, and where they are inspired to do their best work. They are the architects of a better future, building structures that stand the test of time, their foundations rooted in integrity and purpose.

The Intangible Impact: Shaping the World

But perhaps the most enduring legacy of these leaders is the intangible impact they have had on the world. They have challenged the status quo, pushed boundaries, and inspired others to think differently. They have shown us what is possible when we dare to dream big, to take risks, and to never give up on our passions. They are the ripples in the pond, their influence spreading outward, touching countless lives and creating a wave of positive change.

Their stories remind us that leadership is not just about achieving personal success, but also about serving others, about making a difference, and about leaving the world a better place than we found it. They inspire us to be more than just managers or bosses, but to be true leaders who empower, inspire, and uplift those around us. They are the guiding stars, their light shining brightly even in the darkest of nights, reminding us that there is always hope, always a path forward.

A Call to Action: Creating Your Own Legacy

As we conclude this exploration of leadership's complexities, let us remember the importance of nurturing our own flames, of continuously seeking growth and self-improvement, and of never giving up on our dreams. Let us strive to create a legacy that we can be proud of, a legacy that inspires others to reach their full potential and make a positive impact on the world. Let us plant the seeds of our own greatness, nurture them with care, and watch them blossom into a legacy that will endure.

The legacy of inspirational leaders is a powerful reminder that our actions matter, that our choices have consequences, and that we all have the potential to make a difference. Let us embrace this responsibility, let us lead with passion and purpose, and let us create a world where everyone can thrive. Let us be the architects of our own destinies, the captains of our own ships, and the authors of our own legacies.

The journey of leadership is not a solitary one. It's a relay race, where each generation passes the baton to the next, ensuring that the flame of inspiration continues to burn brightly. In the next chapter, we will explore the importance of paying it forward, of mentoring and empowering the next generation of leaders, and of ensuring that the legacy of inspiration continues to shape the world for generations to come. The torch is passed, its flame flickering but unwavering, ready to ignite a new generation of leaders.

The Unquenchable Spirit

Throughout this journey, we've explored the complex and often challenging path of leadership. We've witnessed the rise and fall of inspirational leaders, the insidious nature of demotivation, and the transformative power of reclaiming one's passion and purpose. We've journeyed from the blazing bonfire of inspiration to the cold ashes of mediocrity, and back again, witnessing the resilience of the human spirit and the enduring power of leadership.

We've seen how the brightest flames can flicker and fade, how the most driven individuals can succumb to complacency, and how the once-clear vision can become obscured by doubt and uncertainty. We've also witnessed the devastating impact of demotivated leadership, the toxic ripple effect that spreads throughout teams and organizations, leaving a trail of disengagement, low morale, and declining performance. We've seen the once-mighty oak wither and the once-proud ship run aground, their crews lost and disheartened.

But amidst the challenges, we've also seen the resilience of the human spirit, the unwavering determination to overcome adversity, and the transformative power of self-reflection and reinvention. We've witnessed leaders rise from the ashes, reclaiming their passion, reigniting their purpose, and inspiring others to do the same. We've seen the phoenix take flight, its wings ablaze with renewed fire, and the once-dormant volcano erupt with a vibrant display of life.

We've seen how the renewed flame of a leader can create a ripple effect of positivity, engagement, and high performance, transforming not only their own lives but also the lives of those around them. We've learned that leadership is not just about achieving results, but also about empowering others, fostering a culture of collaboration and continuous improvement, and leaving a lasting legacy of inspiration and impact. We've witnessed the transformation of barren landscapes into thriving ecosystems, of dissonant melodies into harmonious symphonies, and of lost souls into empowered individuals.

Key Lessons: Navigating the Leadership Journey

As we conclude this exploration of leadership's complexities, let us remember the key lessons we've learned:

- **The Importance of Self-Awareness:** Recognizing the signs of demotivation and taking proactive steps to address them is crucial for maintaining effective leadership. *The compass must be constantly monitored, the sails adjusted, and the course corrected to ensure the ship stays on track.*

- **The Power of Purpose:** A clear vision and a strong sense of purpose are essential for inspiring and motivating others. *The North Star must shine brightly, guiding the way through even the darkest of nights.*

- **The Value of Continuous Growth:** Embracing challenges, seeking out new experiences, and committing to lifelong learning are key to staying

engaged and avoiding complacency. *The journey is*

not about reaching the summit, but about the climb

itself, the lessons learned, and the growth achieved

along the way.

- **The Impact of Positive Influence:** A leader's

  passion, enthusiasm, and commitment to excellence

  can create a ripple effect that transforms teams,

  organizations, and even communities. *The single*

  drop of water can create a wave of change, its impact

  felt far beyond its initial point of origin.

- **The Responsibility of Paying it Forward:**

  Empowering the next generation of leaders through

  mentorship, guidance, and support is essential for

  ensuring the continued success and growth of our

society. *The torch must be passed, its flame burning brightly, illuminating the path for those who follow.*

The Unquenchable Spirit: A Call to Lead with Passion and Purpose

Leadership is not a destination, but a journey. It's a journey filled with challenges, setbacks, and moments of doubt. But it's also a journey of growth, fulfillment, and the opportunity to make a real difference in the world. It's a journey worth taking, a path worth forging, a legacy worth creating.

So, let us embrace the challenges, let us learn from our mistakes, and let us never give up on our dreams. Let us lead with passion, purpose, and an unquenchable spirit, inspiring others to do the same. Let us be the beacons of light, the guiding stars, the architects of a better future.

The world needs your leadership, now more than ever. Go ahead and make your mark.

Final Thoughts: The Enduring Flame

Remember, the flame of inspiration may flicker, but it can never be extinguished. It resides within each of us, waiting to be rekindled, to illuminate our path and guide us towards a life of purpose and fulfillment. Let us nurture that flame, let us fan its embers, and let us share its warmth and light with the world.

For in the end, it is not the accolades or the achievements that define us, but the lives we touch, the difference we make, and the legacy we leave behind.

www.ingramcontent.com/pod-product-compliance
Lightning Source LLC
Chambersburg PA
CBHW022108210326
41521CB00029B/328